Back to the Blitz

HISTORY SPIES

Jo Foster ha
discovered t
in 1980s Ess
she has ma
programmes
Team and *Wh*

Jo lives in
housemates,
she grows up

If I was a kid with a time machine, I'd want Jo Foster to be my guide. She has an insatiable historical curiosity, treats both the past and t has a mischievous s smiling throughout

Look out for

HISTORY SPIES: ESCAPE FROM VESUVIUS
HISTORY SPIES: THE GREAT EXHIBITION MISSION
HISTORY SPIES: SEARCH FOR THE SPHINX

Back to the Blitz

HISTORY SPIES

JO FOSTER

ILLUSTRATED BY SCOULAR ANDERSON

MACMILLAN CHILDREN'S BOOKS

7/11
799

First published 2009 by Macmillan Children's Books
a division of Macmillan Publishers Limited
20 New Wharf Road, London N1 9RR
Basingstoke and Oxford
Associated companies throughout the world
www.panmacmillan.com

ISBN 978-0-330-44899-4

3 5 7 9 8 6 4

A CIP catalogue record for this book is available from the British Library.

Typeset by Perfect Bound Ltd
Printed and bound in the UK by CPI Mackays, Chatham ME5 8TD

Picture credits:
The Trustees of the Imperial War Museum, London: pages 30, 66, 95, 105 and 131
The National Archives: pages 8, 12, 13, 23 and 63
istockphoto: pages 48, 82, 92, 101, 110, 114, 120, 124 and 125
Dan Newman: pages 15, 25, 91 and 98
Liverpool City Council: page 11

To my parents

Once upon a time, my life was almost as boring as yours.

Then on my birthday last year I got a phone call; it was a bloke from the Department for Historical Accuracy. See, the government had invented a way to go back in time. They wanted someone to travel around and check up on what really happened in history. And they picked me. Probably because of my astounding talents and unusually large brain, I expect.

Since then I've been travelling through time, spying on the craziest stuff. Battles and magicians and feasts and duels. All sorts!

And now you're coming along too, and you're with the best guide around. I'll make sure you get to see everything that's worth seeing!

I'll show you what to wear, what to eat, where to go, how people have fun, where they live – everything. Stick with me and almost nothing can go wrong.

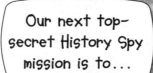

Department for Historical Accuracy

HISTORY SPY 00001

NAME CHARLIE CARTWRIGHT

CLEARANCE ULTRA

Pass must be carried at all times when on official missions. Not valid without stamp.

HISTORY SPIES · DEPARTMENT FOR HISTORICAL ACCURACY

Our next top-secret History Spy mission is to...

ENGLAND
LIVERPOOL
1940

If you want to be a History Spy, you have to keep secrets. You have to keep your eyes open all the time, and remember everything, and most of all you have to be invisible. I don't mean like magic-cloak invisible. The best way to be invisible is to look just like everyone else.

Like if you go to the football, you have to know what to wear, where to stand and what to shout.

Stand in the right end and you're invisible.

Stand in the wrong end and EVERYONE will notice you.

First up, we really need to sort your clothes out. No way am I going to 1940 with you dressed like that. They'll think we're complete fruitloops!

Luckily for you, I'm the greatest Master of Disguise around. Pick some clothes out from this lot:

Cap – not just second-hand, eighth-hand by now

Ribbon – tatty, for tying up hair

Shirt – don't bother ironing it

Cardigan – at least one button missing

Shorts – because trousers are for grown-ups

Shoes – worse for wear

Sandals – to be worn with socks

Long woolly socks – itchy

It doesn't look like much, I know. But it's the perfect kit for an agent on a covert mission. We'll look completely ordinary dressed up like this, so we'll be able to play in the street, get lost in crowds and generally sneak around doing important espionage. Brilliant!

Titfers of 1940*

Anyone travelling to 1940 should wear a hat. These are just a few of the styles you could sport:

TRILBY: Wear this if you're an adult man and you want to cut a sharp figure.

STRAW HAT WITH RIBBON: This one would be good for a little girl in the summertime – but don't wear it out in the rain!

ARP WARDEN'S HELMET: Part of the uniform of an ARP warden. Wear it if you want to wander round during air raids, getting a good (but risky) look at what's going on.

* Rhyming slang. Titfer = tit 'fer' tat = hat

CROWN: Only wear this if you're the King. Unlikely to be much use for most History Spies, but you never know…

HEADSCARF: If you're a grown-up woman you might be wearing one of these to work. Lots

of women work in factories during the war, when the men are away fighting. This will keep your hair clean and out of the way.

BASEBALL CAP: This is definitely wrong. On no account wear one of these until at least 1980.

Make-do and mend

You won't fit in if all your clothes are shiny and new. Because there's a war on, there aren't enough new clothes around, so the government's telling everyone to 'Make-Do and Mend'. You can patch up your shorts, wear your sister's hand-me-downs, or unravel a worn-out jumper and knit a new one. There's no shame in being a bit scruffy in 1940.

Oh, you'll need this too... You can open it later.

MEND AND MAKE-DO TO SAVE BUYING NEW

MAKE-DO AND MEND

ISSUED BY THE BOARD OF TRADE

Did you know that teenagers were only invented in the 1950s? Crazy, isn't it? So when you travel to 1940, you're either a child or an adult, there's no in-between. You just become a man or a woman about the time you leave school and get a job, probably when you're fourteen.

HINT: There's a clever way to tell if someone's a grown-up: look at their legs. Boys wear shorts and girls wear skirts with socks. Then when you become an adult you start wearing long trousers, or skirts with stockings, just like your parents. Weird fashions for rebellious teenagers don't exist yet.

Well, you look just about acceptable now, but before we hit the streets there are a few more vitally important things you should know. Pay attention to the next bit, kid, or you'll get us into all kinds of trouble.

Vital background briefing

The essential quick-reference guide for any History Spy travelling to 1940. Keep this with you at all times!

Liverpool in 1940

Liverpool is the second biggest port in the UK (after London). It's particularly important in 1940 because so many ships leave from here to move soldiers, weapons and food all around the world.

KEY TO MAP
- **Ⓐ** Lime Street railway station
- **Ⓑ** Wapping Dock (destroyed by bombs in 1940)
- **Ⓒ** Grafton ballroom
- **Ⓓ** Liver Building
- **Ⓔ** Hospital
- **Ⓕ** Meccano factory
- **Ⓖ** Liverpool Fire Brigade HQ
- **Ⓗ** Maternity Hospital, Oxford St – where a rock 'n' roll baby was born
- **Ⓘ** Littlewoods' Walton Hall Avenue factory – it's been turned into a factory to make Wellington bombers
- **Ⓙ** St Luke's Church
- **Ⓚ** Head Post Office
- **Ⓛ** Lewis's Department Store

Obviously all our journeys are necessary, because we're on a government mission.

Getting around

There are lots of ways to travel around Britain in 1940. But the war has made everything more difficult. Petrol is rationed right from the start of the war, so transport gets tougher and more expensive.

Fewer trains, trams and buses run during the war. As well as the shortage of fuel, there's a shortage of people to drive them. And there are also more people moving around the country than in peacetime. Soldiers are being taken to Europe, kids are being evacuated to the countryside, women are going to work on the land. So with fewer trains and more people, you'd better be prepared for a squash when you're travelling in 1940. It also costs three times as much to take a train in wartime.

This is why the government's put up posters telling people to use Shanks' pony to get around.

Actually, 'Shanks' pony' is another way of saying 'your legs'. It just means you should walk short journeys. Or you could get a bike and go anywhere you like. But remember, watch out after dark!

Where am I?

It's very easy to get lost in 1940.

As a History Spy, you should always make sure you have a good map with you to find your way around the country. In 1940 the government thinks the Germans are about to invade Britain. So they've taken down all the signs on main roads to confuse the Germans when they get here. There are no signs at railway stations either. You can't buy decent maps in the shops. Even buses don't say where they're going on the front. You could try stopping someone to ask directions. But people are being told not to help others who are lost, in case they're spies. There's a really annoying rhyme that children are being taught in school:

'If anyone stops me to ask the way,
all I must answer is "I can't say".'

Luckily, the Germans never do invade – but all this confusion makes life even more difficult for History Spies.

Funny money

Some History Spies find the money in 1940 confusing. It's actually very simple. In 1940, there are:

> *240 pence in every pound instead of 100*
> *Every pound (£) has 20 shillings (s)*
> *Every shilling (s) has 12 pence (d).*

So 12 x 20 = 240. There are other words you need to get used to, like 'crown' (5s), 'guinea' (21s) and 'bob', which is another word for a shilling.

If you see something for sale at 2 shillings and 6 pence, the price tag will look like this: 2/6d. You can also call that 'half a crown', or 'two and six'.

Practise this – you'll be spotted very quickly if you get it wrong.

I still mess this up. I always forget how many sixes in 240. Everyone must be much better at maths in 1940. Nobody has a calculator either...

A 1940s phrasebook

1940 isn't that long ago, but there will be words you don't understand at first. This list ought to help.

And remember: watch your mouth. History Spies must never use modern slang. If you call things 'wicked' or 'minging', people will be very suspicious.

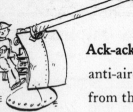

Ack-ack – an anti-aircraft gun. They get their nickname from the sound they make. Anti-aircraft guns are set up in parks and playing fields, and they try to shoot down bombers as they fly over.

All clear – the note that sirens play when an air raid's over. When you hear the 'all clear' it's safe to come out of your shelter.

ARP – stands for 'Air Raid Precautions'.

Black market – buying and selling things illegally, without ration stamps

Blitz – the bombing raids on British cities. It comes from the German word 'Blitzkrieg', or 'lightning war'.

Bobby – policeman

Bomber's moon – when the moon shines brightly enough to show the bombers where to aim

Browned off – bored, fed up

Chap – a person (usually a man or boy)

Crikey/cripes – wow!

Dogfight – a mid-air fight between aeroplanes

Evacuee – someone who has been moved to the countryside, out of the way of the bombs

Jerry – nickname for the Germans

Keep mum – keep quiet. Also means 'don't gossip'.

Ollies – marbles

POW – prisoner of war

RAF – Royal Air Force

Ration book – a book of coupons showing how much food you're allowed to buy. You'll get very hungry in 1940 without one.

Rotter – a mean person

Spiv – someone who sells things on the black market

U-boat – a German submarine

WAAF – Women's Auxiliary Air Force

Wireless – the radio

Wizard – brilliant

WRNS – Women's Royal Naval Service

WVS – Women's Voluntary Service

And whatever you do, don't forget to adjust back again when you go home. Last time I came back from 1940 I told one of my mates he was a 'wizard chap'. Everyone took the mickey for weeks. What a load of rotters!

Take me to your leader

Who's running the country in 1940?

King George VI and Queen Elizabeth

- George VI is King from 1936 to 1952.
- George is small and shy. He didn't really want to be King – it should have been his brother Edward's job, but Edward had already given up the crown.

> Anyone would think it was no fun being King. Maybe I should apply if no one else wants the job.

- George has a bad stammer, but still makes speeches. People like this because it shows he's brave.
- Even Buckingham Palace gets bombed in September 1940.
- This King and Queen have a daughter you might know better: she grows up to be Queen Elizabeth II.

Winston Churchill

■ Winston Churchill is Prime Minister from 1940 to 1945.

■ He's famous for smoking big cigars.

■ His hobby is bricklaying. When he gets stressed, he builds walls to calm down.

■ Churchill's wife called him 'Mr Pig'. In a nice way.

■ When Winston was a little boy, his teachers thought he was stupid. He was always late and always in trouble. He still grew up to be one of Britain's greatest Prime Ministers. ← So there's hope for all of us, the

■ The grown-up Churchill is famous for making great speeches. They really cheer everyone up during the war (see p. 49).

■ Churchill was fun to be around, and had some famous friends. In the 1930s he had both Charlie Chaplin AND Albert Einstein to stay at his house.

How to avoid arrest

Remember, History Spies who break the law risk getting arrested. And getting arrested could put the whole future of the government's time travel programme in danger. It's also pretty unpleasant for you.

There's a new law which says that you can be executed for spying. So watch it!

All kinds of strange things are illegal in wartime as well. You could be prosecuted for:

● 'making defeatist remarks' – if you think the war's going badly, keep your mouth shut!
● hoarding more food than you need
● icing a cake – it's a waste to put sugar on a cake as well as in it.

- letting any light out of your house in the blackout (see p. 71 for more information)
- making unnecessary journeys
- talking about where your son or brother is. If they're in the army, navy or RAF, and if enemy spies overhear you, they might be able to work out where the British are going to attack next.

If you're outside in the blackout, be careful – there are robbers about when the streets are dark! Crime's risen in wartime, and some burglars are making a good living looting houses that have been hit by bombs. If you see anyone doing this, report them to a policeman at once.

Now we've got to be careful, because it's a risky situation in 1940. It's the middle of the Second World War. Remember what I said about keeping secrets? Well, if anyone finds out we're 'spies', they'll think we're enemy spies and they'll throw us into prison. And then we'll have to bend time and disappear, and we'll have changed history, and it will all be very embarrassing, Ok? So keep shtum. Like the poster says. It's telling people not to talk about important war stuff, because there might be German spies listening.

You can open up that cardboard box now, if you like. It's your gas mask. Everyone in 1940 has one. There are even special bag-type masks you can fit your whole baby inside and gas masks for dogs! The government is expecting the Germans to fly over and drop poisonous gas on us at any moment. It's OK, they never do.

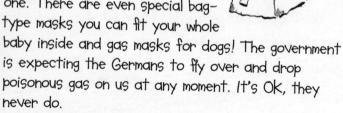

Gas masks are horrible to wear. They smell of rubber and they make some people feel trapped. But for us History Spies they can be useful – they're an excellent disguise.

See – try and spot me in this crowd!

Remember to keep your gas mask safe. Air-raid wardens can check on it, and if you've lost it you'll have to pay a fine.

You'll need one of these too: an identity card. Fill it in before you go, and keep it safe.

NATIONAL REGISTRATION IDENTITY CARD

NOTICE

FF 185525

1. Always carry your Identity Card. You must produce it on demand by a Police Officer in uniform or member of H.M. Armed Forces in uniform on duty.

2. You are responsible for this Card, and must not part with it to any other person. You must report it at once to the local National Registration Office if it is lost, destroyed, damaged or defaced.

3. If you find a lost Identity Card or have in your possession a Card not belonging to yourself or anyone in your charge you must hand it in at once at a Police Station or National Registration Office.

4. Any breach of these requirements is an offence punishable by a fine or imprisonment or both.

FOR AUTHORISED ENDORSEMENTS ONLY

These cards were brought out specially because of the war. This proves you're a British citizen. Police constables can ask for your ID card at any time. They're checking for spies, so don't get caught!

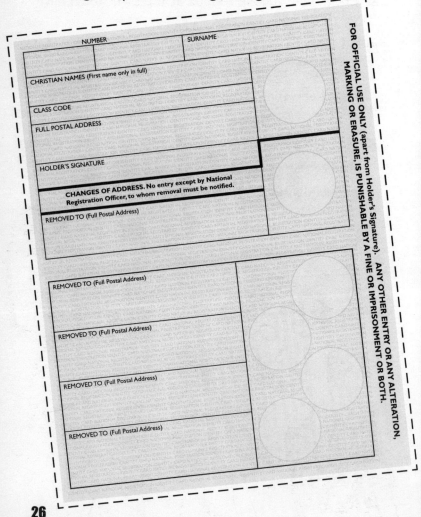

Things to absolutely _not_ do, ever!

- Check your mobile to look at the time. You'll have to ask somebody, or find a clock.
- Take your contact lenses out in front of anyone. They have been invented, but most people won't have seen them before. So if you do wear lenses, keep it to yourself.
- Mention your holiday in Tenerife. The only people who go abroad these days are soldiers, and ordinary people definitely don't get to go on aeroplanes.

Imagine how much it'd freak you out if you saw someone taking the front of their eye off. Gross!

Let's go and have a look around... Hey, check out that queue – it's mammoth! Bet there's something worth having for sale at Lewis's. That's the big department store around here. If we're lucky they might have something really special like bananas. Come on, let's get in line and see if we can find out.

Why all the queues?

Everywhere you go in 1940, you'll see huge queues. Just going shopping for your tea can take hours! The problem is, there's not enough of anything to go round.

... and here we are. Liverpool, 1940. Magic, hey?

The German troops are after our bananas. They know that Britain needs food and supplies from abroad, so German submarines (called U-boats) are attacking British ships at sea. It's hard for ships to get through, whether they're carrying guns, oranges, clothes or whatever. So for now we can only get things that are made in Britain, and not very much of them.

Because there aren't any supermarkets, you have to go to lots of different shops. You queue up at the butcher's to get your meat. Then you go to the greengrocer's and queue up to get your veg. Then you queue at the fishmonger's to get your fish...

Basically, you could spend all day standing in queues. And if you complain you'll hear everyone's favourite phrase in 1940: 'Don't you know there's a war on?' They use it to explain absolutely everything that goes wrong.

You'll see this sign a lot in 1940. There's a song about a greengrocer which goes 'Yes! We have no bananas, we have no bananas today!' Shops put it in their windows as a joke – but it's true too. Most people don't even see a banana for the whole of the war.

"Yes we have No Bananas"

I don't know about you, but I've had enough of queuing. I think we deserve some fun. My nan always says she made her own entertainment when she was a girl. We'll give it a go, shall we?

These guys are playing marbles – it's called 'ollies' round here. Hey chaps, mind if we join in?

How to win at 'ollies'

You will need:

● a mate to play with
● some 'ollies': marbles with stripes of coloured glass inside
● a space outdoors

That's all!

How to play:

1) Look closely at your ollies to decide how much they're worth. An ollie with one colour inside is a 'one-er', if it has two colours it's a 'two-er', and so on.

2) Make sure you both agree on this – you don't want arguments later.

3) Player 1 throws his ollie a short distance.

4) Player 2 tries to hit it with her ollie. If she hits it on the first go, and if it's a 'one-er', then she's won and she gets to keep Player 1's ollie.

5) If Player 1's ollie is a two-er or more, the game goes on. So if it's a 'three-er', Player 2 needs to hit it three times in a row to win. If she misses, it's Player 2's go.

6) Player 2 now has to throw her ollie and let Player 1 try to hit it. Keep going like this until someone's won all the other person's ollies.

If you're a good player, you can get loads of ollies and be the envy of all your friends.

Other games you could play in the street to make friends include skipping, leapfrog and hopscotch. Or, if you can find a ball, football.

Sport

You can watch a lot of the same sports in 1940 as you can back home, although there have been changes because of the war. Like the cinemas, theatres and dance halls, sports stadiums closed down in 1939 when the war started. When they opened again soon after the end of the war, things were very different. There's less of all kinds of sport, because the men who play it have gone off to fight, and because sporting events use up valuable petrol, money and energy.

FOOTBALL

● The football league's suspended for the war. This is good news for Portsmouth fans – they keep the FA Cup for seven years, from 1939 to 1946!

● The slimmed-down War Cup is introduced instead in 1940. The first winners are West Ham, who win 1-0 at Wembley.

● Lots of clubs lose players because they go off to fight. Almost all the Arsenal squad have joined up to go to war.

● Football's as popular as it is back home, but the crowd sizes are limited in wartime. You'll have to queue, like for everything else!

CRICKET

■ There's even rationing on cricket in 1940. The only kind you're allowed to play is one-day cricket.

PRISONERS STOP PLAY

■ If you try to go to the Oval in London to watch cricket, you'll be disappointed. It's being used as a Prisoner of War camp.

■ Tennis is hit too: the Home Guard are doing weapons training at Wimbledon.

■ At Twickenham, the Rugby Union headquarters have been turned into allotments.

OLYMPICS CANCELLED

■ The Olympic Games were due to be held in Helsinki, Finland in 1940. But the Finns are a bit busy just now – they're fighting the Russians. The Olympics will have to wait until after the war, when they're held in London in 1948.

A dead cert

Psst! This is completely illegal. History Spies aren't allowed to bet on the horses. But it can't be that wrong if we only bet a little bit, can it? I've been looking through some old newspapers and I've got a hot tip. On 6 April, Bogskar wins the last Grand National to be held during the war. It all happens at Aintree racecourse, near Liverpool. We could go and see him in action – if you don't mind bending the rules, that is...

Ecstatic crowds greet

rival of Bogskar in the winner's enclosure yesterday at Aintree's Grand National

39

At the pictures

To blend in, History Spies working in 1940 should try to go to the cinema regularly. Tickets cost a few pence[*] and you get loads for your money. For example:

A ten-minute newsreel telling you what's going on in the war

★★★

One or two cartoons, maybe starring Donald Duck, Mickey Mouse or Bugs Bunny

★★★

A 'B-film', which is a short film or maybe a documentary

★★★

The main feature film

Don't be surprised if people behave a bit differently in a 1940 cinema. You're allowed to smoke, and it can get rowdy if there are lots of young kids in.

[*] *Don't forget – 'd' is the sign for pence.*

NOW SHOWING
GONE WITH THE WIND

The number one film of 1940. People queue round the block for this all through the year. It's an extremely soppy love story which makes everyone's mum cry. You'd better get a comfy seat for this one, it's 3 hours and 40 minutes long! If you make it to the end, you can spot Clark Gable saying the famous line 'Frankly, my dear, I don't give a damn'.

WARNING: Features kissing, crying, etc. Yuck!

LET GEORGE DO IT

George Formby is a comedian from Wigan. He sings daft songs and plays an instrument called a 'banjolele'. His catchphrase is 'It's turned out nice again'. In this film, he has a dream where he flies to Germany, tells Hitler to 'put a sock in it', and then punches him on the nose. It's best to join in when the audience cheers at this bit!

BROADWAY MELODY OF 1940

Starring Fred Astaire, this is packed full of big dance numbers. It'll make you want to learn to tap dance.

FLASH GORDON CONQUERS THE UNIVERSE

Zooming Off The Earth! Skyrocketing Through Space! Starring Buster Crabbe as Flash Gordon, this film sees the superhero battling the evil Ming the Merciless to save the world from a terrible disease: the Purple Death. Finally, some real action! It's not exactly X-Men, but it's still my favourite 1940 film.

Oh no, whenever I come to the pictures it's **always** Gone with the Wind! It's dead slushy — let's get out of here before the smooching starts.

Trekkers

Guess what these people are up to.

a) They're off on holiday.

b) They're going for a picnic.

c) They're moving house.

Wrong – they're **trekkers**. They're off to stay in the countryside.

Trekkers are people who don't want to stay in the city at night because of the bombs. Or sometimes, trekkers have already been 'bombed out' – that's when your house is hit in an air raid. Either way, they walk right out of the city every evening with all their stuff. And next morning you'll see crowds of them trekking back in to go to work. And to think people from our time complain about commuting!

I've got a friend down this street who we can trust. She's my best friend in 1940. I've tried telling her I'm a History Spy but she thought I was joking, so don't say anything about it, eh?

Come on, I'll introduce you – it's time you met some 1940 people properly. You can have a look round an ordinary house, and we might even get some dinner. Remember you're supposed to be a 1940s kid though – stay in character!

Home, Sweet Home

We're lucky, we've got our own Anderson shelter in the garden. At first I thought it was quite fun, like having a Wendy house. But the rain gets in and it's full of spiders.

Every night, me and Mum go round pinning the blackout curtains back up. They're really heavy.

46

There's no TV in 1940. Hardly anyone can afford a television, but even if you do have one it's no use. The BBC switched off the TV signal in 1939 because of the war.

> Still, at least almost everyone has a radio – oh sorry, I mean a wireless.

There are only two channels on the wireless: the Home Service and the Forces' Channel. If you don't like what's on those, you're stuck!

Pearl's mum's favourite programme is a comedy show called *It's That Man Again*. It stars a famous Liverpool comedian, Tommy Handley. History Spies may find it helpful to learn some of the catchphrases from this show:

> Don't forget the diver!

> Can I do you now, sir?

> Lovely grub!

> Trust me – people in 1940 will think you're hilarious.

Other radio programmes include:

● **Children's Hour with Uncle Mac:** only lasts thirty minutes due to wartime shortages! Features short stories, songs, and classic serials like *The Wind in the Willows* and *Great Expectations*. Uncle Mac always ends the show with his catchphrase: 'Goodnight, children everywhere.'

● **Charley McCarthy:** Charley's the name of a ventriloquist's dummy.

Yes, this really is a ventriloquist's show on the radio. (Come on... think about it!)

As well as comedy and music, you can sometimes hear the Prime Minister make a speech on the wireless. He makes people feel they know him and can trust him. When he makes a speech, seven out of ten people in Britain tune in!

Test yourself: which of these things did Winston Churchill NOT say in 1940?

'I have nothing to offer but blood, toil, tears and sweat'

'We shall fight on the beaches'

'This was their finest hour'

'Oh pants, it's not going very well, is it?'

'Never in the field of human conflict was so much owed by so many to so few'

But the most important thing people listen to on the wireless in 1940 is the news...

And now: the news

In wartime the news is very important, and there's a lot of it. Everyone wants to know how the war's going. Half of all the adults in Britain listen to the news at 9 o'clock every night.

You'll notice one thing missing from the news in 1940: the weather. Weather forecasts are banned in case German pilots listen in and find out what conditions are going to be like.

In October 1940, BBC Broadcasting House in London was hit by a bomb during the 9 o'clock news. A muffled crash went out over the radio, but the newsreader carried on talking even though he was covered in dust!

Radio announcers and newsreaders are big stars in the 1940s. Still, the job isn't quite as glamorous as before the war. Until 1939, newsreaders had to wear dinner jackets and bow ties to work in the evening, so that they looked smart at all times.

I don't get it. How would anyone know, on the radio?

Of course, you could always buy a newspaper if you miss the news on the wireless. You can get all of these papers in 1940:

The Daily Mirror

The Daily Mail

Daily Express

Picture Post

The Observer

THE TIMES

The **Daily Express** is especially popular. And children like it because it features Rupert the Bear cartoons.

STOP PRESS
THE BATTLE OF BRITAIN

In Summer 1940, the 'Battle of Britain' is being fought in the sky over south-east England. The German forces are planning to invade Britain. They know that first they need to beat the RAF (Royal Air Force), otherwise their ships will never make it across the Channel without being bombed. So for nearly four months, aeroplanes are shooting at each other in mid-air. When the Luftwaffe (the German air force) are beaten in October, Britain will know that it's safe from invasion.

The RAF pilots become heroes during the Battle of Britain. People start calling the pilots 'The Few', because they're a small number of men who save the whole of Britain from being invaded. The fighting is so dangerous that during the Battle of Britain these brave young pilots are only expected to live for a few weeks.

When planes fight each other in mid-air, it's called a dogfight. History Spies visiting Britain in 1940 can head to south-east England for the best views of the fighting.

> I saw a dogfight once – it's so exciting! It's like a cross between a 3D war film and a Red Arrows display!

But ... why is there a war on anyway?

Adolf Hitler had been planning a war since he became Chancellor of Germany in 1933. He thought Germany had got a bad deal at the end of the First World War, and he wanted to get back the land that had been taken away from Germany. Hitler took over the National Socialist German Workers' Party (you probably know them as the Nazis). He built up the army, navy and air force, and used them to start attacking the countries around him. First he moved his troops into the Rhineland, then he took Austria, then Czechoslovakia.

Mussolini, the Italian dictator

Hitler

People in Britain couldn't decide whether Hitler would stop if they just let him have a bit more land to keep him happy, or whether he was so dangerous that they should go to war to stop him. Britain and France decided that they would have to stop Hitler if he invaded Poland – and then he did. The war began on 3 September 1939.

Friend or enemy?

1940 is pretty early in the war. Not everyone's taken sides yet. Be careful not to make mistakes in conversation – follow this handy guide.

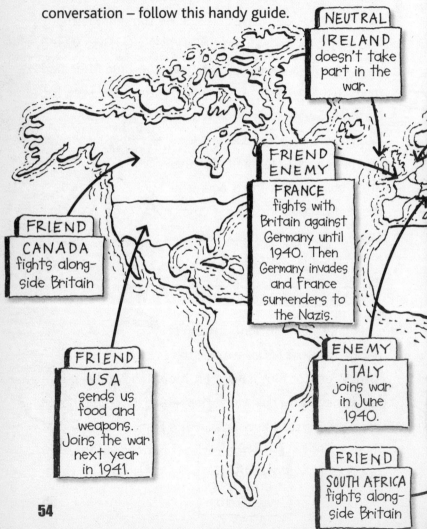

NEUTRAL
IRELAND doesn't take part in the war.

FRIEND ENEMY
FRANCE fights with Britain against Germany until 1940. Then Germany invades and France surrenders to the Nazis.

FRIEND
CANADA fights along-side Britain

FRIEND
USA sends us food and weapons. Joins the war next year in 1941.

ENEMY
ITALY joins war in June 1940.

FRIEND
SOUTH AFRICA fights along-side Britain

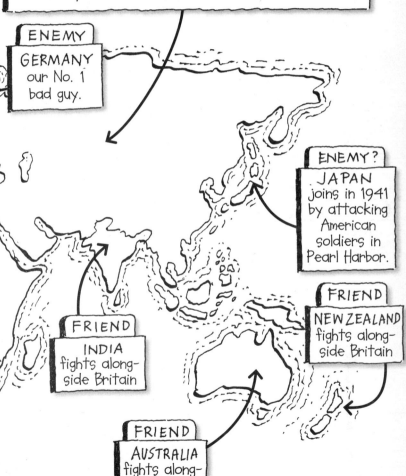

Friends behind enemy lines

All over Europe, countries like Poland, France and Czechoslovakia are being taken over by Germany. But many people in those countries are still fighting against the Germans. They know they'll be killed if they're caught, so they're working together in top-secret 'underground' groups.

France has the most famous resistance movement. Almost all the French postmen work for the Resistance, forwarding messages and passing on German orders to the British. French railway workers blow up trains and tracks to stop German supplies getting through. People who are resisting the Nazis in Europe start using the 'V' symbol to show what they think. 'V' stands for 'Victory', and people paint Vs all over the place, on walls and pavements. Or even easier, you can make it with your fingers.

Tea with Pearl

Well, Pearl's mum's invited us to stay for tea, and it would be rude not to. But I warn you, the food isn't exactly the best thing about 1940.

Menu

Sparrow pie

No sausages cos meat's rationed. But there are always loads of sparrows around!

Cabbage, carrots, potatoes

Stewed prunes

Yuck – I think this is supposed to be dessert

Have as much as you like – veg comes from the allotment

Yum! Fried crow again!

Yes, the food in 1940 is pretty repulsive. How do you fancy some fried crow? If you can catch it, you can eat it!

Or maybe you'd rather try seagull stew with a side order of stinging nettles cooked in margarine? Or carrot jam on your bread at teatime? Or if you fancy something really gruesome, how about brains on toast or baked stuffed sheep's heart?

Still, things are going to get worse after 1940. By the end of the war they'll be eating whale meat, and you really don't want to try that! It tastes like old boots polished with fishpaste.

For a treat, kids sometimes get 'connie-onnie butties'. You take two slices of bread and stick them together with super-sweet gloopy condensed milk. Yummy!

FAIR SHARES

Because there's not enough food for everyone in the country, the government's introduced rationing in 1940. Everyone has a ration book, with coupons to say how much of each food they can buy. You'll need this book with you whenever you go shopping, or you'll get pretty peckish!

Each week, an adult is only allowed to buy this much of the following things:

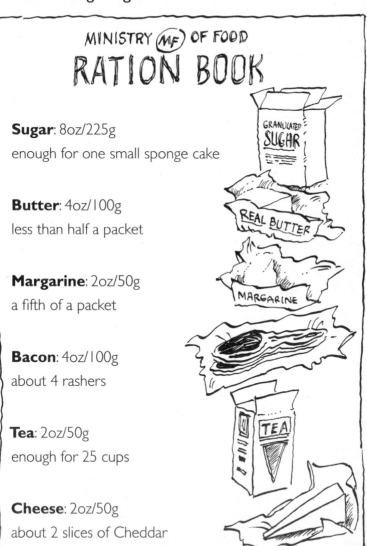

MINISTRY (MF) OF FOOD
RATION BOOK

Sugar: 8oz/225g
enough for one small sponge cake

Butter: 4oz/100g
less than half a packet

Margarine: 2oz/50g
a fifth of a packet

Bacon: 4oz/100g
about 4 rashers

Tea: 2oz/50g
enough for 25 cups

Cheese: 2oz/50g
about 2 slices of Cheddar

Imagine... you could have a cheese and pickle sandwich and that's all your cheese used up for a whole week. Oh well, no one's heard of stuffed crust pizza in 1940 anyway, so maybe they don't know what they're missing.

You can eat as much as you can get of these things:

Vegetables (parsnips, potatoes, carrots, spinach...)

Offal (liver, kidneys, stomach)

Yay! Unlimited stomach!

Bread

Fish – if you can get it. Like other boats, the fishing boats are being attacked by Germans, so you won't find much fish in the shops.

Chicken – but you won't find much. All the chickens are being kept alive for their eggs.

EGGS ONLY

If you're eating out as a History Spy, look out for the 'Communal Feeding Centres'. They're restaurants run by the government so that if people have run out of coupons, they can still get a healthy dinner. You can buy a hot meal for about 1 shilling and sixpence.

It's not exactly 5-star cuisine, but it's better than nothing.

COMMUNAL FEEDING CENTRE

Dig for victory!

Because there's not much food, the government is encouraging everyone to grow their own vegetables in their gardens or allotments. These posters go up all over the place: even the moat of the Tower of London has been dug up to plant veg.

You could even try to 'grow your own' meat. There are 'Pig Clubs' which you can join, to look after a pig with your neighbours so that you all get some bacon when it's killed. In the countryside, more people start keeping rabbits. They're not really pets though – more like future pies!

It's easy to get your 'five a day' when there's little to eat except veg. People are especially keen on potatoes. Over the page are two 1940s recipes that show how you can make all sorts of 'tasty' treats out of spuds.

Whenever I try making them they taste foul, but maybe you'll do better...

DIG FOR VICTORY

POTATO PANCAKES

- ◆ 1 lb /450g mashed potatoes
- ◆ $\frac{1}{2}$lb / 225g cooked carrot
- ◆ Milk
- ◆ Salt
- ◆ Pepper

Whip the mashed potato to a loose creamy consistency with a little milk. Season well with salt and pepper, add diced cooked carrot. Pan-fry slowly in very little fat until crisp and brown.

POTATO CHOCOLATE SPREAD

- 2 tbsp mashed potato
- 1 tbsp cocoa
- 1 tbsp sugar
- Vanilla essence

Mix the cocoa, sugar and flavouring into the mashed potato. Use as a spread instead of jam.

I really hate the food in 1940. The longer I stay here, the hungrier I get, and I always come back skinnier!

All right for some

Everybody had to learn to live with rationing in 1940. Even the King and Queen have ration books. But Winston Churchill manages to stay chubby all through the war. He's exempt from rationing, and eats whatever he likes – and drinks plenty of champagne too!

One day in 1952, Churchill asked to see what the rations were like for everyone else in the country. He had a look at a week's rations, and said it looked fine to him. The only problem was, he thought it looked like enough food for one meal, not one week.

Reduce, re-use, recycle

Everyone's going recycling mad in 1940. It's not because they're worried about saving the planet. It's because there just isn't enough of anything to go round, so nobody can afford to waste anything. Recycling is all part of the 'War Effort'. Housewives are handing in all their saucepans to be made into Spitfires.

Kids can join gangs of 'Cogs' who go round their neighbourhoods collecting rubbish for recycling.

You can recycle paper, rubber, bones, milk-bottle tops, toothpaste tubes . . . and any leftover food goes to feed pigs, so even your bacon butty's recycled!

Follow the lines to put these everyday items through the Recycling Mangle:

RUBBER

ANIMAL BONES

TOOTHPASTE TUBES

AEROPLANES

BOMBS

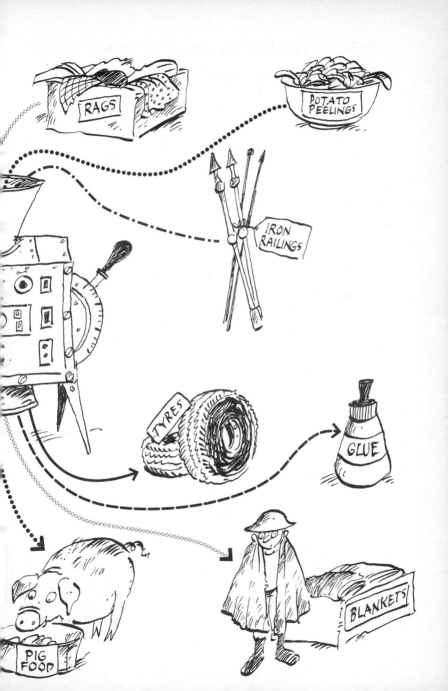

Hey – who turned the lights out?

It's dangerous to drive around without headlights, but in 1940 it can be even more risky to have the lights on. When German planes fly over the country, they're looking for cities to bomb. Lots of lights would make the cities easy to spot. So during the bombing, the 'blackout' means that everyone has to block out all the lights in their houses and on their bikes and cars, and of course the street lights are out too. It's hard to imagine if you live in a twenty-first-century city where it's never dark.

Blackouts can be useful for History Spies, because you can sneak around without being seen. But watch out for holes in the road, cats to tread on, lamp posts to bump into, and most of all for cars and lorries! There are twice as many deaths on the roads in the first month of the war as in any normal month.

Just like cyclists now, people in 1940 wear reflective gear so they can be seen in the blackout. Women can buy luminous fake flowers to wear. And don't be afraid if you're in the countryside and you see a big ghostly glowing cow coming towards you. Farmers have been painting their animals white to stop cars crashing into them.

This is the
ARP uniform

History Spies who don't mind the dark and want to do some night-time snooping could try dressing up as an ARP warden.

Part of the warden's job is to go round checking that there's no light coming from any houses. Everyone has to put thick blackout curtains in their windows every night, or cover them with black paper. And if there's a raid and the warden's neighbourhood is hit, he has to help the fire brigade and report the damage.

I'm going to enjoy coming back to 1940 when I'm a grown-up. They get all the best outfits!

Practice makes perfect

If you're going to stay in 1940 for a while, you'll need to learn to prepare your house for the blackout. Try this before you leave: cover up one of the windows of your house. You could use black cloth, black binbags or black paper... either way be careful not to leave any gaps or you might get into trouble. Can you get it so that someone in the street wouldn't see even a tiny chink of light?

It's trickier than you think. I filled in the gaps with a black permanent marker when I tried, back at home. My dad wasn't very impressed.

Put that light out!

This is what you'll hear if an ARP warden sees any light coming from your house. Wardens won't let you get away with anything. One garage owner was fined for switching on a neon light. Fair enough if it had been night-time, but this was in the middle of the day...

Now **this** is a nice bright place to go in the blackout. The Grafton ballroom. It's where Pearl's big sister Fran goes to dance with her mates. Look how huge it is – it can hold 1,200 people. It's state-of-the-art too; it's got a special springy floor for bouncier dancing! Here, I'll give you a leg-up so you can have a sneaky peek through the window...

GET IN
THE SWING

Are you an alligator, a hep-cat,
a rug-cutter or a tin-ear?
Get down the Grafton
and find out!*

THE
GRAFTON

* By the way... an alligator, a hep-cat
and a rug-cutter are all people who are
into swing music. A tin-ear is someone
who can't stand it.

77

The Jitterbug is the latest and hottest dance from America. You do it to swing music – Glenn Miller's 'In The Mood' is a great tune for this kind of dance. History Spies who can jitterbug well will always find friends in a dance hall, so practise it before you go.

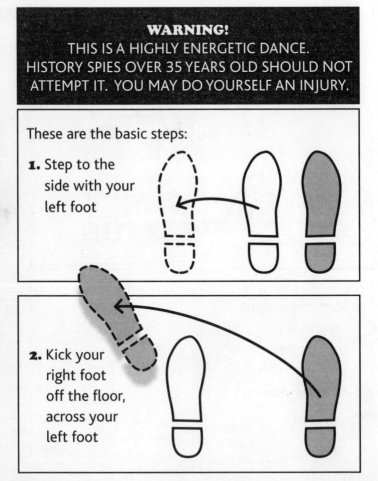

WARNING!
THIS IS A HIGHLY ENERGETIC DANCE.
HISTORY SPIES OVER 35 YEARS OLD SHOULD NOT
ATTEMPT IT. YOU MAY DO YOURSELF AN INJURY.

These are the basic steps:

1. Step to the side with your left foot

2. Kick your right foot off the floor, across your left foot

3. Place your right foot
to your right side

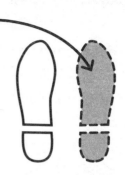

4. Stamp your left foot

5. Stamp your right
foot, then turn your
body so your partner
is on your right side
and lean sideways.

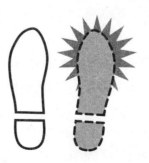

Once you've mastered these steps, try some wilder moves:

The Peck: Push your chin forward over your partner's shoulder; then straighten up to face your partner; repeat. Makes you look a bit like a chicken.

The Peabody Hop: Jump on both feet; kick your right foot between your partner's feet; jump on both feet; kick your left foot outside your partner's feet; jump on your left foot; jump on your right foot. Be careful always to jump on to your own feet – not your partner's.

The Charleston Kick: Stand side by side with your partner, holding hands and with your free hands swinging. Step forward with your left foot; bend your left knee; kick your right foot off the floor, straightening your left knee at same time. Bend your left knee. Turn to the opposite direction, step forward on right foot ... and continue until you're exhausted.

More advanced dancers lift their partners over their heads and do backward somersaults over each other. They'll even throw in some quick rounds of leapfrog, or suddenly do the splits. DO NOT try these moves at your first dance!

Keep practising, and soon you'll be a real Jitterbug – or if you're a girl, a Scobo Queen (sounds bizarre, but it just means you're good at dancing).

The 1940 chart show

Everybody loves a good tune, whatever the year, and History Spies should familiarize themselves with the hits of the day so they don't seem out of touch.

Music's important for keeping people cheerful when things get rough in the war. There are love songs, dance tunes, songs to sing along to when you're working, and songs to make you feel braver. More people than ever are listening to classical music, and there's lots of it on the BBC. But you're most likely to hear the 1940s version of pop songs. You might have heard of some of these before:

In the Mood – to get you on the dance floor

A Nightingale Sang in Berkeley Square – a slow, slushy one to make you cry

You Are My Sunshine – a bouncy one to cheer you up

There'll Always Be An England – a stirring, patriotic one for keeping your spirits up

But storming in at number one is…

We'll Meet Again

This famous tune is sung by the 'Forces' Sweetheart', Vera Lynn. It's about people going off to war and saying goodbye to their loved ones. If you hear this song in 1940, try singing along – here are the words:

We'll meet again
Don't know where
Don't know when
But I know we'll meet again some sunny day

Keep smilin' through
Just like you always do
Till the blue skies drive the dark clouds far away

So will you please say hello
To the folks that I know?
Tell them I won't be long
They'll be happy to know
That as you saw me go
I was singing this song

We'll meet again
Don't know where
Don't know when
But I know we'll meet again some sunny day

eeeeee—EEEEE!!

Wheeee—eeeeeeee

Oh pants – I mean 'crikey!' – is that the time?! It's the air-raid siren. The German planes are coming over to bomb the city.

Quick – DUCK!

Just kidding! Sorry, mate. But you should have seen your face! You should trust me more. I've checked it out and if we head for St Luke's Church we won't meet any bombs tonight.

Whenever there's an air raid people head down to the crypt, underneath the church. It's where the old tombs are, and it's a bit spooky, but once it fills up with people you'll hardly notice the ghosts!

Mind the bombs

✳ Sirens are a warning that someone has spotted German planes coming over to bomb the city. This is called an air raid.

✳ One of the first air raids on a British city takes place in Liverpool, in August 1940.

✳ London is first bombed on 7 September 1940.

✳ People call the air raids 'The Blitz' after the German word for 'lightning war': Blitzkrieg.

✳ The blackout is supposed to hide cities from the German planes flying overhead. There are even fake cities popping up in the countryside. People build huge bonfires to fool the bombers into attacking fields instead of real factories.

✳ If possible, History Spies should always check with the records to find out when their area was bombed. Then you can just avoid the dangerous parts of town. But if you do get caught out in an air raid, the safest place to be is underground.

* Lots of people in 1940 have air-raid shelters in their back gardens, like Pearl did. You have to build an Anderson shelter yourself from one of those kits where some bits are missing and the instructions don't make sense. Some Anderson shelters are pretty flimsy, and they're often damp. Still, at least there's space to grow vegetables on top.

* If you don't have a garden, you can get a Morrison shelter to put up inside your house. It's a big steel cage, about the size of a double bed. It works pretty well as long as you don't mind sleeping in a giant rabbit hutch.

* Other families just hide under a sturdy table. This is a good option if your house doesn't have a shelter.

* If you don't have a home in 1940, or you're outdoors when the siren sounds, go to a public shelter.

* In London, people start buying tickets for the Tube and just stay there all night. It's a very safe place to be because the tunnels are so deep. In Liverpool there's no Tube so people find other underground hide-outs, like the church crypt.

✴ Other Londoners turn into cavemen. People set up home in Chislehurst Caves in Kent, and get the train to work from there.

✴ The Blitz Spirit: It's not cool to admit you're scared of the bombs. People are very proud of 'fighting back' against the Blitz by not acting afraid.

✴ The Blitz doesn't just happen in Liverpool and London. If you're travelling in time in another city, check this map first to see if your city is in danger.

KEY

1	Bath	13	Ipswich
2	Birmingham	14	London
3	Bristol	15	Manchester
4	Bury St Edmunds	16	Newcastle
5	Cambridge	17	Norwich
6	Canterbury	18	Nottingham
7	Cardiff	19	Plymouth
8	Clydebank	20	Portsmouth
9	Coventry	21	Sheffield
10	Exeter	22	Southampton
11	Great Yarmouth	23	Sunderland
12	Hull	24	Swindon
		25	York

Mustn't grumble

It seems odd to make a joke of being bombed, but that's just what a lot of people in the war do. It helps them stay cheerful when the war gets depressing.

There's one joke going round about an old woman in an air raid. She wouldn't go down to the shelter because she couldn't find her false teeth. Her son tried to persuade her, saying 'Come on – they're dropping bombs, not sandwiches!'

These signs have all been put up on businesses and shops that have been bombed:

BLAST!

No window cleaners need apply

Open as usual but more open than usual

Be good – we're still open

A star is born

If you hang around the right part of Liverpool in October 1940, you could hear something special. Listen out for a new baby crying in the Maternity Hospital on Oxford Street. It might just be John Lennon. He's born on 9 October in the middle of an air raid. He'll grow up to be in the Beatles, the biggest pop group of the twentieth century. Come back and see him in the 1960s and he'll be rich and famous!

He's a bit young to be giving out autographs, I guess... We could try to get him to dribble on something for us.

Pets under fire

People don't just worry about getting hurt in an air raid themselves – they're also looking out for their pets. If you've got a cat or a dog, you'll know how scared they get on Bonfire Night. You have to keep them indoors away from all the noise. Well, in the war people have the same problem all year round. Some people try sticking cotton wool under their dogs' ears and tying their ears down with cloth. And to make sure pets aren't left behind after an air raid, the RSPCA hands out cards to put in your window saying whether you've got a dog or cat. So hopefully, if your house is bombed, the fire brigade will try to dig your dog out from the wreckage as well as the rest of your family.

The world's biggest Christmas dinner

On Friday 20 December 1940, there was an air raid which hit the docks very hard. Because some of the warehouses were filled with turkeys for Christmas, they all got roasted in the fires – which made it the tastiest-smelling air raid in history.

Phew! It's morning. See, I told you there wouldn't be any bombs here. They all fell on the docks last night instead. D'you want to go and look?

Liverpool's the second biggest port in Britain. In the war, ships go from here to take soldiers and sailors all around the world on dangerous missions. Then there are all the ships coming in with supplies of food and weapons. Whenever you see one arriving, you have to think of the other boats that didn't make it. Lots of them will have been sunk by German submarines or planes. Many men you'll meet in Liverpool are sailors and it's a really risky job, especially during the war.

I definitely wouldn't be brave enough.

And look at that boat. It's getting ready to go to Canada. It's not taking soldiers or weapons, it's taking a load of kids. Most kids from the cities are going by train to safe places like Wales, but some get an even bigger adventure. They're being sent abroad (Canada, Australia, New Zealand or South Africa) with CORB, the Children's Overseas Reception Board. It's not as safe as it sounds, because even evacuee boats can be bombed or torpedoed. And if you do get through safely you have to start up a whole new life in a foreign country, away from all your family and friends.

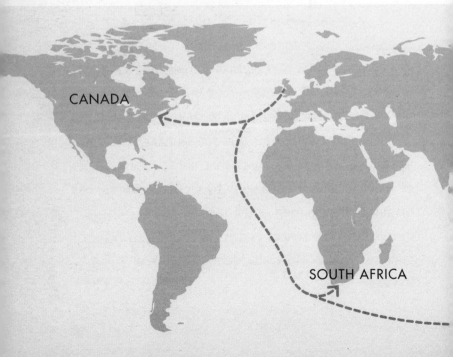

CANADA

SOUTH AFRICA

Spitfire spotting and bits of bomb

WILLS'S CIGARETTES

BRISTOL "BLENHEIM" BOMBER

WILLS'S CIGARETTES

HEINKEL He. III BOMBER

ALBUMS FOR WILLS'S PICTURE
CARDS CAN BE OBTAINED FROM
TOBACCONISTS AT ONE PENNY EACH

SPEED

A SERIES OF 50

9

SUPERMARINE "SPITFIRE"
FIGHTER

Although no exact performance
figures can be quoted for the Supermarine "Spitfire" single-seat fighter,
which is in production and will
shortly go into service in the R.A.F.,
it is definitely the fastest fighting
aeroplane in the World. The "Spitfire" is a low-wing cantilever mono-
plane. It has one 1,050 h.p. Rolls-
Royce "Merlin" II 12-cylinder
liquid-cooled motor, and is officially
described as a multi-gun fighter. It
was designed by Mr. R. J. Mitchell,
who designed the Supermarine S-6B
seaplanes which gained the Schneider
Trophy outright for Great Britain.
The World landplane speed record is
at present held by the German Messerschmitt fighter (Card No. 10), but
a special version of the "Spitfire"
may break this record before long.
(*By courtesy of "The Aeroplane"*).

W. D. & H. O. WILLS
MANUFACTURERS OF GOLD FLAKE, CAPSTAN,
WOODBINE AND STAR CIGARETTES
BRANCH OF THE IMPERIAL TOBACCO CO.
(OF GREAT BRITAIN & IRELAND).

Before the war, kids used to swap cigarette cards.
Cigarette packets had picture cards inside them, and
you'd try to collect the whole set. But now there's
something far more exciting to collect. Whenever a
German plane's shot down, or after an air raid, you
might find bits of plane or bomb lying around. Everyone
collects this stuff, but it's a really dangerous hobby.
Don't touch it – several kids have been hurt when
they picked up unexploded bombs by accident.

Collecting shrapnel isn't the only way for careless kids to get horrible injuries. During the Blitz, all kinds of buildings suddenly get opened up and turn into playgrounds. Bombed-out houses are great for climbing on, running around in, smashing up... But they also have a habit of falling down on kids who play in them.

Plane spotting is another new hobby. History Spies should learn how to tell different aeroplanes apart so they can fit in. You get extra points for spotting a German bomber!

If it's flying low enough, you can tell whether a plane's German or British by its markings. This cross means it's the Luftwaffe, the German Air Force...

WILLS'S CIGARETTES

B.F.W. MESSERSCHMITT Bf. 109 FIGHTER

And these rings are for the British RAF...

WILLS'S CIGARETTES

HAWKER "HURRICANE" FIGHTER

But mostly, you won't be able to see these marks, so you'll have to learn to identify planes by their shapes.

BRITISH PLANES

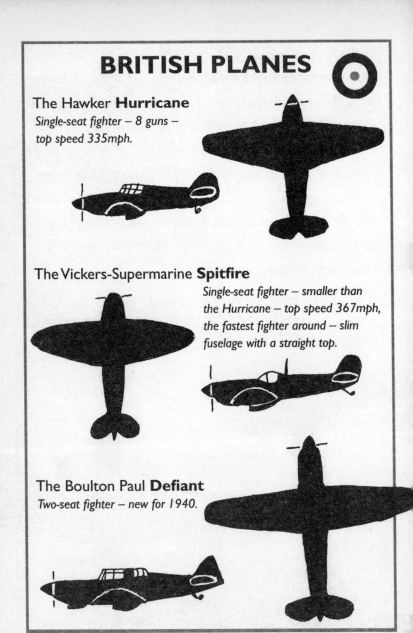

The Hawker **Hurricane**
*Single-seat fighter – 8 guns –
top speed 335mph.*

The Vickers-Supermarine **Spitfire**
*Single-seat fighter – smaller than
the Hurricane – top speed 367mph,
the fastest fighter around – slim
fuselage with a straight top.*

The Boulton Paul **Defiant**
Two-seat fighter – new for 1940.

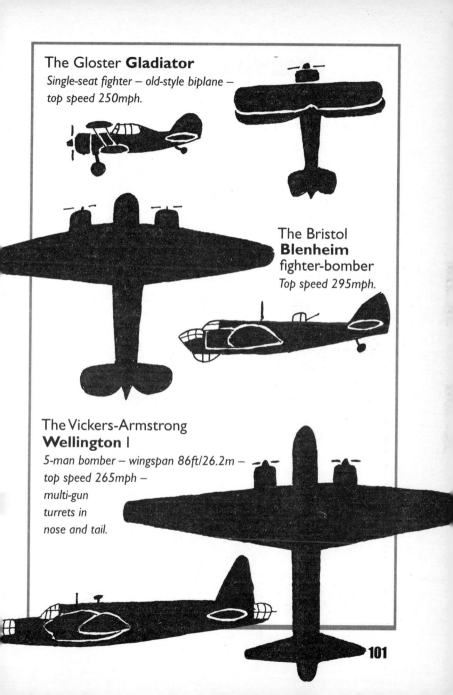

The Gloster **Gladiator**
Single-seat fighter – old-style biplane – top speed 250mph.

The Bristol **Blenheim** fighter-bomber
Top speed 295mph.

The Vickers-Armstrong **Wellington** I
5-man bomber – wingspan 86ft/26.2m – top speed 265mph – multi-gun turrets in nose and tail.

GERMAN PLANES

The **Heinkel** He 111k

4-man bomber – upper surfaces and sides black, underneath grey-blue – wingspan 74ft 3in/23m – top speed 274mph – the Luftwaffe's standard long-range bomber, often used to attack North Sea shipping.

The **Dornier** Do 215

3-man reconnaissance bomber – wingspan 59ft 2in/18m – top speed 312mph – 3 movable machine guns – look out for its bulbous nose, twin fins and twin rudders.

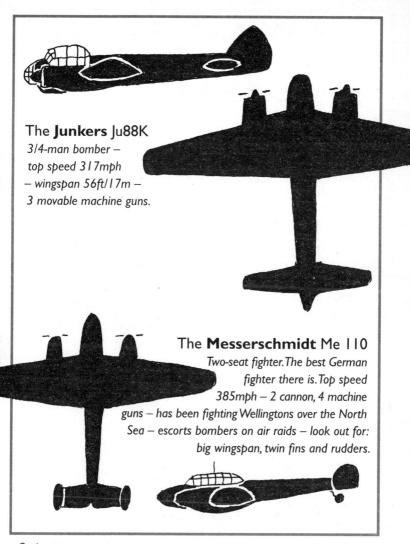

The **Junkers** Ju88K
*3/4-man bomber –
top speed 317mph
– wingspan 56ft/17m –
3 movable machine guns.*

The **Messerschmidt** Me 110
*Two-seat fighter. The best German
fighter there is. Top speed
385mph – 2 cannon, 4 machine
guns – has been fighting Wellingtons over the North
Sea – escorts bombers on air raids – look out for:
big wingspan, twin fins and rudders.*

Got all that? Good. It's useful to know your planes so you can tell if a bomber's one of ours or not. But also, you're no one in the playground if you don't know a Spitfire from a Messerschmidt.

Speaking of the playground, I bet you weren't expecting to see many other kids around, huh?

Evacuate! Evacuate!

At the start of the war, the government knew the Germans would probably bomb British cities. So they drew 'danger areas' and 'safe areas' on a map of the country. They planned to move children, their mothers and pregnant women from the danger areas to safe places before the bombing started. This big people-shifting plan was called evacuation.

When the war started in September 1939, 85,000 people were evacuated from Liverpool in just a few days. By January 1940, more than a third of them have come back. This is because there were no bombs for the first few months of the war. Some people send their children away again after the raids start. In May 1941, there will be a severe attack on Liverpool which is called the 'May Blitz', and lots of parents send their kids away after that.

Obviously, most people didn't want to split up their families. Some people felt it was better to stay together even if you were going to be bombed.

You know what, though? I reckon there are days when my dad would love to send me away to the countryside for a year or so. I wonder if anyone sent their kids away just for the peace and quiet?

The government tried to persuade everyone that the cities were too dangerous for children – they even had vans going through the streets with loudspeakers on top, telling people to sign their kids up for evacuation.

Happy ever after?

So what did the government decide to call their grand plan? Operation Safe Haven, perhaps? Operation Country Living? Even just Operation Evacuation? No, they went for Operation Pied Piper. Yes, that's right – after the Pied Piper of Hamelin, the fairytale musician who steals a whole town's worth of children and never brings them back. It doesn't sound like they expected the evacuation plan to go very well.

> So, d'you fancy trying out this evacuation thing? Come on then... I've got some instructions here somewhere.

Kid swap

First, you'll need to pack a small suitcase.

What to take:

- one change of clothes
- soap
- a toothbrush
- your ID card
- your ration book
- your gas mask
- a luggage label with
  your name and
  address, to tie
  to your clothes
  so you don't
  get lost

I feel like a bit of abandoned luggage wearing this thing...

Once you're sure you look the part, join up with a school group at Lime Street station. From there, you'll be put on a train to a faraway place like Shropshire or Wales. Grown-ups like teachers and priests will go with you to look after you.

Obviously we History Spies are experienced travellers. But the person you're pretending to be may never have been away from home before. Real evacuees won't even know if they'll ever see their parents again.

I'm an evacuee...
Get me out of here!

When you get to the 'safe area', you'll be taken to a place like the local village hall. Then the local people come along and choose the evacuees they want to take home. Expect to be prodded, asked questions and left until last if you look dirty, ill or just ugly. You might get your hair washed, combed for nits and maybe cut short, because people in the countryside assume the city kids will be dirty.

Phew! After that journey I'd definitely be the last to be picked. I look a right mess! Not as bad as you, though.

Seems like some kids have a great time in the countryside ... others aren't so lucky.

The man I'm staying with never cleans his house - it's disgusting, there are rats everywhere!

Cawn 'n anfonedig at deulu i mewn Gogledd Cymru a ond areithia Cymraeg. Cawn at ddysg 'n chwim.*

I'm staying with a rich old lady, in a big house with servants. I think she hates me, but the food is great!

I got picked by a farmer - I have to milk the cows every morning and do chores around the house whenever I'm not at school!

It's OK... but I can't get used to how quiet it is at night in the country.

* I got sent to a family in North Wales who only speak Welsh. I had to learn quickly.

When they're evacuated, everyone gets given one postcard and a free stamp. This is so they can write and tell their family they're OK as soon as they get to their new home.

I hate writing letters, but even I wouldn't be this bad. This is a real-life postcard from a boy to his mum. She must have been so worried.

POST CARD

FOR CORRESPONDENCE

FOR ADDRES

ILF
1 -P
9 SE
1940
DEVO

Dear Mum,

I hope you are well.

I don't like the man's face much. Perhaps it will look better in daylight.

I like the dog's face best.

Tom

Mrs Wa

242 Atte

Toxteth

Liverp

A bad Friday 13th

Not all evacuees get sent to the countryside in trains. As you saw at the docks, some are shipped off to America and Canada instead. Those children won't see their parents again for the whole of the war.

But the evacuee ships stop in September 1940. On Friday 13th an unlucky ship leaves Liverpool, and is hit by a German torpedo a few days later. After that, sending children all the way across the Atlantic doesn't seem such a safe bet.

y Street

17 SEPTEMBER 1940...

600 MILES WEST OF

IRELAND: PASSENGER SHIP

'CITY OF BENARES' HIT

BY U-BOAT. MANY DEAD

Weird evacuees

It's not just kids who are evacuated in the war. All sorts of people and things are being moved around the country . . .

■ Two giant pandas and a bunch of other exotic animals have been moved from London Zoo to Whipsnade in Bedfordshire.

- The Bank of England has moved from London to a little village in Hampshire.
- The most expensive paintings in the National Gallery are hidden deep inside a slate quarry in Wales.
- Over 5,000 prisoners have been let out of jail.
- Thousands of sick people have been sent home from hospital, to make room for people hurt in air raids.

School's out

Now this is one thing that's MUCH better in 1940. It's not like our time, when even if you're a government agent on a secret mission people still think you have to be in school every day. Humph!

When the children get evacuated, schools are too. Some schools closed at the start of the war while their air-raid shelters were being built. Also, there's a shortage of teachers in 1940 because a lot of the male teachers go away to fight.

How lucky are they? I think I'm going to go part-time at school when I get home. I might show up on Wednesdays and Thursdays.

This adds up to too many kids and not enough schools! The children who are left behind in the cities often don't have to go to school, or they might only have to go for half or a third of the day. Some children get jobs instead. Others just run around the streets all day.

If you go to a posh private school, you might be out of luck – they have enough money to build shelters and keep going, and the boarding schools are mostly in the countryside anyway. So you might not get any time off at all.

But at least you can leave when you're fourteen!

History Spies who do go undercover in schools will find them very different in 1940 from in peacetime. Teachers aren't allowed to use whistles or handbells in the playground any more, in case people hear them and think it's an air raid warning. Schools cut pencils and notebooks in half because there aren't enough to go round. And school holidays go haywire too, because saving on heating and lighting in the school building is so important when there's not enough fuel. Sometimes a school will give the pupils just two weeks' summer holidays, but then ten weeks for Christmas! It makes for a lot more school holidays with rubbish weather and nothing to do.

Holidays

CANCELLED TILL FURTHER NOTICE

Life can be a lot less fun during the war.

Christmas

SLIMMED DOWN

Christmas is still celebrated, but there's not much food around. There's not enough fruit for the Christmas pudding, and not enough sherry to cheer up your gran. And don't expect any good presents this year either.

Bonfire Night CANCELLED

Who wants to watch fireworks when there are bombs exploding in the streets every night? And anyway, all the gunpowder's being used for weapons.

The seaside CLOSED

You could try going to the beach, but you'll have to watch out for barbed wire and landmines. The beaches are closed, especially on the south and east coasts. Everyone's expecting the Germans to arrive by boat any time soon, so the beaches are ready for battle.

Cheer up though – you can still go on holiday. No one's going abroad, of course. But hiking holidays are very popular. People like getting out of the cities and going somewhere quiet for a change. Or you could go on a working holiday on a farm, like the government are asking you to. Lots of men who used to work on farms have gone to war, and Britain's trying to grow as much food at home as possible.

Honestly, the work never stops in 1940. You know, I think we should head back to the city. It may be dangerous, but at least you don't have to get up close and personal with any cows. If we stick around the countryside it's only a matter of time before some farmer gives us a shovel and a pile of poo to move.

Here, I'll get us a comic to read for the journey back. Look, it's a 1940 Dandy, so it's got Hitler in as well as Desperate Dan!

I can't believe Dan's been eating cow pie for all this time. You'd think he'd be sick of it.

The funnies

Comics are more popular in 1940 than in the twenty-first century. It's not just the *Beano* and the *Dandy*. There's also *Chips*, *Rover*, *Hotspur*, *Film Fun* – even *Radio Fan* for all the news about your favourite wireless programmes.

Contrary to popular belief, cutting two eyeholes in a comic is NOT a recommended technique for spying. Any History Spy who tries this in public will be given a formal warning. You will also look ridiculous.

However, you can use a comic as an excellent cover for hanging around listening to other people's conversations. Or you can just use it for your own amusement.

Light reading for the blackout

Cheap, pocket-size books are still a new thing in 1940. Penguin started publishing paperbacks in 1935, and now they're really popular. People buy all kinds of novels and non-fiction. Books about politics also sell really well and are useful for agents who are still reading up on 1940. One of the bestsellers for adults this year is *No Orchids for Miss Blandish* by James Hadley Chase. It's a thriller about American gangsters killing each other in nasty ways.

Younger History Spies might enjoy Enid Blyton's books, like the Famous Five series. Or you might like to try some of the Just William books by Richmal Crompton. They're about a scruffy boy who lives in the country in England and is always getting into trouble. *William and the Evacuees* comes out in 1940.

And if you prefer an action story, get hold of a Biggles book. Biggles is an RAF pilot, and in 1940 he stars in *Biggles Secret Agent*.

See, everyone loves a spy story! It's because we're all so cool and daring.

In fact, do you see that guy over there? I reckon he's a spy. See how he's trying not to look like he's taking notes?

Spying on the spies who spy on the spies

Not all spies in 1940 are enemy spies – or History Spies. There's another kind of 'spy' snooping on his neighbours. In 1937 three friends started a group called 'Mass Observation' so they'd know what ordinary people really thought and what their lives were like. People from around the country volunteer to write reports on what's happening in the streets, pubs and buses around them. They're out there now, writing down all kinds of useful gossip about everyday life, like how often people go to the cinema, what they think about the war, and whether they're carrying their gas masks. It's the perfect job for nosy neighbours.

How not to spy

There are a few real enemy spies around in wartime Britain. Some of them aren't very good at staying invisible. Try to avoid these simple mistakes:

- One spy was caught by farmers when he wandered out of the sea, wearing a hat and carrying a briefcase. Maybe he thought he was blending in.
- Another spy was reported by a pub landlord in Kent. He didn't know about pub closing time, so he had to be new to Britain!
- Some people are a bit too keen to catch Germans. When a British pilot parachuted out of his plane over Hampshire, a local member of the Home Guard shot at him!

The spy-catcher's phrasebook

Impress your friends with a bit of German. People in the Home Guard learn these handy phrases in case they ever bump into an enemy spy or a fighter pilot whose plane has been shot down.

How to challenge an invader

Hands up!	Hände hoch! *(Hen-de hohh!)*
Hand over your weapons!	Übergeben sie Ihre Waffen! *(Oober-gay-ben zee ear-uh vaffen!)*
Surrender, or I'll shoot!	Ergeben Sie sich, oder ich schiesse! *(Air-gay-ben zee sish, oh-der ish shee-se!)*
Quick march!	Vorwärts marsch! *(For-vearts marsh!)*
Turn around!	Umdrehen! *(Oom-dre-hen!)*
Left turn!	Links um! *(Links oom!)*
Right turn!	Rechts um! *(Rechts oom!)*

There are also British spies working in their own country, trying to catch enemy spies. Every letter you send abroad in 1940 will be opened and read, and if you write anything that could help a foreign spy your post will be censored. This means that the sensitive bits will be scribbled out, or even cut out of your letter. So if you aren't careful about what you write, your penpal could get a letter that looks like this:

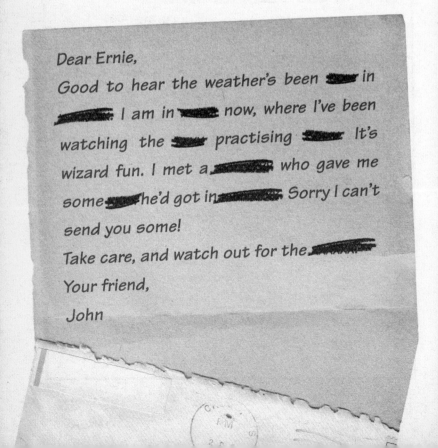

Dear Ernie,

Good to hear the weather's been ▬▬ in ▬▬▬. I am in ▬▬▬ now, where I've been watching the ▬▬ practising ▬▬▬ It's wizard fun. I met a ▬▬▬▬ who gave me some ▬▬ he'd got in ▬▬▬▬ Sorry I can't send you some!

Take care, and watch out for the ▬▬▬▬

Your friend,

John

There are plenty of spies around who don't have glamorous jobs like we do.

But who wants to be a Post Spy when you can be a History Spy?

The postmen spies

In Edge Lane, Liverpool, the old Littlewoods Pools offices have been taken over by MC5, the government's postal censorship service. They spend all day opening people's mail to check there are no enemy spies in England.

One foreign spy was caught out because he wasn't good enough at chess. He'd been sending coded messages disguised as chess moves. But the MC5 agent who read the letter was following the chess game and knew the moves made no sense – so the spy was caught.

Funny foreigners

People in 1940 can be a bit suspicious of foreigners. Now there's a war on, suddenly anyone with a different accent sounds a bit sinister. All over Britain, people from other countries are being locked up in case they might be spies. Outside Liverpool, in Huyton, the government take over a council estate and put barbed wire all round it. It's been turned into a huge prison camp for foreigners. But a lot of the Germans who are kept here are actually Jews and other people who ran away to England to escape Hitler in the first place. Inside the camp, they give each other lectures to pass the time. These are so popular that people start calling the camp 'Huyton University'.

Even if they aren't locked up, foreigners have a hard time. One German man's been fined for owning maps of the British countryside. He thought he had a fair excuse – he's lived in Britain for ages and his hobby is walking. In fact, the poor chap is a member of a rambling club which was set up especially to encourage friendship between the English and the Germans.

There's something very exciting going on near what's now Milton Keynes, and it's going to help Britain win the war. The Germans have invented an encoding machine called Enigma, which is supposed to scramble messages so that the code is unbreakable. So the British government has gathered an assortment of brilliant code-breaking geeks at a top-secret base called Bletchley Park in Buckinghamshire. They pick mathematical geniuses, musicians, even people who are really good at crosswords! The Bletchley Park codebreakers are so clever, they like to relax by playing games of chess... and they don't even need a chess board.

But most of the time, they're working flat out to build a machine which can crack the code of the Enigma machine. When they finally manage it in 1940, it changes the war – the British army now knows where the Germans are planning to attack, and where their submarines are. And they don't just help win the war; the people working at Bletchley Park also play a part in the history of the computer.

These people are amazing! They win the war, they invent computers... they're the coolest geeks ever. They almost make me want to join chess club.

But remember, no one in 1940 knows this is going on. No one at Bletchley Park is allowed to tell anyone what they did in the war for at least the next thirty years. So if you do meet one of the amazing super-brains, you won't know anything about it.

Britain is preparing in other ways too. There's a whole secret army in training at a base somewhere in southern England. They're called the Auxiliary Units. If Hitler had actually managed to invade Britain, these guys would have been a guerrilla resistance army. They're learning to use weapons and to make bombs. But they're also being trained in some weird-sounding unarmed combat, like the Sentry Hold and the Japanese Strangle, and a way to knock a man out using a matchbox or fend him off with a chair.

The Auxiliary Units even have exciting James Bond-style gadgets like the 'Time Pencil'. No, it's not an early transporter for History Spies. It's a fuse for a bomb, disguised as an innocent propelling pencil.

Cool! I want a secret exploding Time Pencil.

Of course, you can't go around filling in your occupation on forms as 'Spy'. We all need 'covers' when we travel back in time. It's easier for kids – we can just hang out and play and go to school occasionally, but adult History Spies have to pick jobs to do. At least there are plenty to choose from.

Working overtime

Pretty much everybody has too much work to do in 1940. This includes some people who wouldn't have had jobs at all before the war.

Women's work

Female History Spies will find 1940 an exciting year to visit. As men go away to fight, women start doing all kinds of important jobs. You could try joining the Women's Land Army to see how farms are run in 1940, fire an anti-aircraft gun and try to bring down a German bomber, drive a lorry or an ambulance, or help find new homes for people whose houses have been bombed. Lots of women go to work in factories and make aeroplanes and bombs.

A spotter's guide to uniforms

This guide will help History Spies to spot who's who in 1940. It's also a guide to what to wear if you want to use a uniform to conceal your identity on a mission.

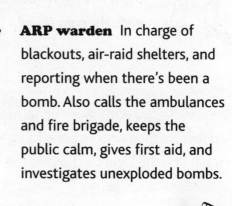

ARP warden In charge of blackouts, air-raid shelters, and reporting when there's been a bomb. Also calls the ambulances and fire brigade, keeps the public calm, gives first aid, and investigates unexploded bombs.

Fireman This job gets especially busy and dangerous during air raids.

British Army Officer The standard uniform worn by the officer classes.

Home Guard Volunteers who train to defend Britain in case Hitler invades. Also known as 'Dad's Army' because they're mostly too old to fight. They don't have much kit either – the lucky ones have khaki uniforms like this. Hardly any of them have guns, because there aren't enough to go round.

Women's Land Army Women who've signed up to work on farms, to replace men who've gone to fight. You'll find the Land Girls out in the countryside.

WVS Women volunteers who turn up at bomb sites with mobile canteens to feed tea and sandwiches to emergency workers.

Policeman If you see one, remember the tips on How to avoid arrest (p. 21).

German airman This is a German uniform. He must be a pilot who's crashed his plane – you should report him to the authorities.

Postwoman Just one of the jobs that women have taken over. You can go around all kinds of places on your own in this uniform and no one will give you a second look.

WREN A woman in the navy. Wrens don't fight, but they can do lots of other jobs, like flying planes.

Sailor There are a lot of sailors in Liverpool because it's such a big port.

A man called Alfred Hancock was arrested during the war for impersonating an RAF officer. In real life, Alfred worked as a labourer at the docks. The court was outraged. They couldn't understand how he'd got hold of an RAF uniform. Easy, Alfred explained. He'd just bought it from a tailor. It's illegal but if you really need a uniform, you can get one. Just don't get caught.

Are you doing your bit?

Kids help out in the war in all kinds of ways. Young History Spies can learn about the war and fit in by doing some of the following things:

- joining local Cadet Forces
- making bandages from old sheets
- cleaning in hospitals
- fire-watching

> This one sounds fun. You're a highly important lookout for the fire brigade, spotting fires as quickly as they start!

- painting kerbs white
- making tea and sandwiches for emergency workers
- knitting hats, scarves and gloves for servicemen and women

WANTED
BOYS WITH PLUCK

If you're a boy aged between 15 and 18, you could sign up for the Liverpool Defence Corps. You'll be trained in first aid, fire fighting, dealing with gas, the effects of high explosives, and the geography of the local area.

It's sort of like being in the Scouts but with added peril!

Here, work it out for me, will you?

Keep your secrets secret

All good spies need a code. If you get a cryptic message while you're working in 1940, use this table to decode it. Just find each letter in the message on the bottom rows of this table, and write down the bold letter above it. So if you find TYG GTYQ, you start by writing down the letter above T, which is A . . . and so on.

T	**I**	**M**	**E**	**S**	**P**	**A**	**B**
Z	Y	X	W	V	U	T	S
C	**D**	**F**	**G**	**H**	**J**	**K**	**L**
R	Q	P	O	N	M	L	K
N	**O**	**Q**	**R**	**U**	**V**	**W**	**X**
J	I	H	G	F	E	D	C
Y	**Z**						
B	A						

Well, what are you waiting for? It sounds like a mission to me! Let's go!

I wonder what these are for? Hang on, I think there's something stamped on the crossbar here...

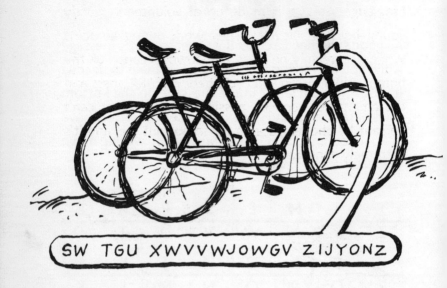

SW TGU XWVVWJOWGV ZIJYONZ

Work it out here:

Whoa...OK. Now I don't want to lie to you. This is a pretty dangerous one. We'll have to go out during an air raid, in the dark, with bombs falling all around us and ambulances whizzing past us. I've heard people get killed doing this job. You sure you're up for this? Well, I just hope you're fast on your bike, that's all!

Solution: BE ARP MESSENGERS TONIGHT

'ARP' stands for Air Raid Precautions — it's the group of people who save lives during air raids. The ARP Messenger Service is made up of volunteers, mostly young boys on bicycles. They work during air raids. When the telephone lines are down because of the bombs, ARP Messengers cycle between ARP posts and the emergency services, passing messages that can't be sent by phone. It's a vitally important job, and it's extremely dangerous.

Hop on then, we've got to get to the ARP post to report for duty!

Finally! You're late! We've had some injuries in the next road. Take this message to the ambulance depot — and quick!

Meanwhile, in the rest of the world...

What's happening outside Liverpool in 1940?

- Penicillin's being developed by scientists from Oxford University. It may taste bad, but it's going to save millions of lives.

- 9 April: Germany invades Denmark and Norway.

- 10 May: Germany attacks Belgium, Holland, Luxembourg and France.

- 10 May: Winston Churchill becomes Prime Minister after Neville Chamberlain resigns.

- 15 May: In America, two brothers open a burger restaurant. Their names are Dick and Mac McDonald, and their business is going to be huge. Super-sized, even.

- 26 May: Dunkirk evacuation begins – hundreds of fishing boats join in with the Navy and cross the Channel to rescue British soldiers stuck in northern France.

- 10 June: Italy declares war on France and the UK.

- 22 June: France surrenders to Germany (and later in June, to Italy).

- 30 June: Germany invades Britain — well, the Channel Islands of Guernsey and Jersey, at least.

- 10 July: start of the 'Battle of Britain'.

- September: the London Blitz begins.

- 12 September: four teenagers (and their dog) exploring in France discover the Lascaux caves, full of amazing cave paintings that are 17,000 years old.

- 28 October: Italy invades Greece.

- 31 October: end of the 'Battle of Britain'.

What happens next?

If you're planning to stick around, you'll need to know what happens in the war after 1940.

1940
1941

YOU ARE HERE

May 1941: Liverpool Blitz – Liverpool's hit harder than ever before.

June 1941: Clothes rationing begins.

22 June 1941: Germany invades Russia.

7 December 1941: The Japanese attack an American naval base at Pearl Harbor, Hawaii. The USA enters the war.

December 1941: Britain helps Ethiopia get rid of the Italians and become independent.

1942

26 January 1942: The first American soldiers to come to Britain (GIs) land in Belfast.

1942

January 1942: Hitler instructs the Nazis to kill all the Jews.

15 February 1942: The Japanese win Singapore from Britain.

2 May 1942: Japan takes over Burma from Britain.

2 October 1942: Battle of El Alamein, North Africa: Britain wins against the Germans.

22 August 1942: Battle of Stalingrad begins. After five months of fighting, the Russians will beat the Germans.

1943

8 September 1943: Italy surrenders to the Allies.

1944

6 June 1944: D-Day: the Allies invade Europe.

1945

January 1945: Whale meat available in the UK.

28 April 1945: Mussolini is executed.

30 April 1945: Hitler commits suicide in Berlin.

8 May 1945: VE (Victory in Europe) Day; Germany surrenders.

1945

July 1945: Churchill loses the General Election and a Labour government take over.

6 August 1945: USA drops an atomic bomb on Hiroshima, Japan.

15 August 1945: VJ (Victory in Japan) Day – Japan has surrendered, and the war is officially over!

July 1948: The NHS (National Health Service) is introduced. Everyone gets free healthcare for the first time.

1948

2 June 1953: Queen Elizabeth II is crowned in Westminster Abbey.

1953

July 1954: End of rationing, finally! All over Britain, people burn their ration books in relief.

1954

ESCAPE FROM VESUVIUS

HISTORY SPIES

Have you ever been on a top-secret, life-and-death, time-bending government mission before?

Pompeii: AD 79

Vesuvius is about to erupt and the Department of Historical Accuracy needs a History Spy with nerves of steel . . .

Your mission: find out what went on at a gladiator battle, why it's OK to burp at a banquet and why everyone in Pompeii was so smelly! Then, if you're brave enough, you can check out the eruption that buried the city for 2,000 years.

Join top History Spy Charlie Cartwright in his adventures as he travels through space and time, dodging bombs, dinosaurs and erupting volcanoes.

A selected list of titles available from Macmillan Children's Books

The prices shown below are correct at the time of going to press. However, Macmillan Publishers reserves the right to show new retail prices on covers, which may differ from those previously advertised.

History Spies: Escape from Vesuvius Jo Foster	978-0-330-44900-7	£4.99
History Spies: The Great Exhibition Mission Jo Foster	978-0-330-44901-4	£4.99
History Spies: Search for the Sphinx Jo Foster	978-0-330-44903-8	£4.99
The Worst Children's Jobs in History Tony Robinson	978-0-330-44286-2	£6.99
How Loud Can You Burp? Glenn Murphy	978-0-330-45409-4	£5.99
Stuff That Scares Your Pants Off! Glenn Murphy	978-0-330-47724-6	£4.99
The Ultimate Survival Guide Mike Flynn	978-0-230-70051-2	£9.99

All Pan Macmillan titles can be ordered from our website, www.panmacmillan.com, or from your local bookshop and are also available by post from:

Bookpost, PO Box 29, Douglas, Isle of Man IM99 1BQ

Credit cards accepted. For details:
Telephone: 01624 677237
Fax: 01624 670923
Email: bookshop@enterprise.net
www.bookpost.co.uk

Free postage and packing in the United Kingdom